To David
& Janet

Oct/04

Much love
your neighbour
forever (in absentia)

Jeanne
Jorgensen

A Piece of Egg Shell

*An Anthology of Haiku
and Related Work*

Magpie Haiku Poets

ISBN 0-9734761-0-9

CONTENTS

FOREWORD

I had the privilege of meeting with each of
these six Magpie Haiku Poets and sharing
haiku on a regular basis for a period of about
a year and a half when I was living in Alberta.
I was struck by the consistent seriousness and
humor in their approach to haiku and to life.
That intriguing combination is seen in this
characteristic haiku by Tim Sampson:

enough room
between the gravestones
barrow full of leaves

Is this graveyard humor? Enough room for the
never-ending fallen leaves to be dumped
somewhere past the ever-increasing fallen
humanity. Life must go on and even the dead
must give way sometimes.

The frailties and needs of one's own feelings
can serve as a focus on that borderline between
humor and pathos, as in these haiku by Joanne
Morcom, Lesley Dahl and Jean Jorgensen:

winter night
I keep the telemarketer
talking

talking to myself
one red maple leaf
stops it all

new calendar
absently... she flips ahead
to spring

Also found in this collection are haunting
scenes that still our hearts, as in these examples
0by Patricia Benedict and DeVar Dahl:

through the blizzard
a small boy marches
shouldering an icicle

prairie wind
snow fills the mouth
of the badger hole

It is fitting that this group has named itself
the Magpie Haiku Poets. When in Alberta
I spent many hours observing this wonderful
bird. Maligned by many for its opportunist
appetite but acknowledged as the most
intelligent North American bird after the crow,
its humor struck me the most:

empty pop bottle
cocking its head for a look
magpie

Let us hope that, like their namesake, the Magpie Haiku Poets continue their perceptive and humorous look at this world and that they continue to share these often heart-stopping moments with us for years to come.

Bruce Ross

INTRODUCTION

It may have been Schopenhauer who discovered or decided that there are only two ways to penetrate through the suffering and absurdity of existence: through the pursuit of aesthetics or the path of the ascetic. For those who tend to agree, but who don't want to have to choose between these two methods, there is haiku.

The ascetic nature of haiku is readily apparent. Haiku are impoverished in length, limited in vocabulary and restricted in form and subject matter. Haiku poets agree to make these sacrifices, and the Zen roots of haiku ask them to give up one more thing: the self. They are encouraged to abandon values, emotions, worries, expectations and ideas, and leave behind only the world and a pen or pencil.

What can result is an uncanny beauty. The experience of haiku is not like the experience of other poetry, but is, rather, akin to the memories and direct encounters of our lives. This is the aesthetic of haiku. And lo and behold, we do penetrate the absurdity of life, but we step not into some transcendental realm, but into the midst of trees, bugs, sidewalks, wind, and we meet the occasional magpie. We encounter the grand trappings of our everyday existence.

We are lucky it is only the self and not the individual that dissolves into the haiku moment; otherwise we wouldn't have this collection from the Magpie Haiku Poets. Here we have six individuals who, through their varied responses to the "here and now" are able to reveal so many of the truths held in a moment. By actually becoming part of that moment and not simply observers, these poets create the intimacy that makes their haiku both evocative and accessible for the reader.

The title of the collection is taken from one of the entries by DeVar Dahl:

easter snow
a piece of egg shell
in the sandwich

In his classic style, reminiscent of the old masters, DeVar leaves little doubt where the "here" is or when the "now" is happening.

He also quietly suggests the interconnectedness of things, in this case through their whiteness. There are some people who would notice this connection and smile, and there are some who wouldn't notice at all. We are fortunate that there are some like DeVar who notice, and are willing to share their insight with the world.

Along with this interconnectedness, the Zen spirit of haiku reminds us that things are always changing:

they seem to drift
out of waning moonlight
snow clouds

This work by Jean Jorgensen again shows us the importance of quietly paying attention, probably the most valued skill of a haiku poet. If we neglect this, the world will pass us by like a drifting cloud. By paying attention, we can enjoy the company of that drifting cloud as it passes by.

There is an ongoing non-debate among members of the Magpie Haiku Poets around the distinction (or lack thereof) between senryu and haiku. Our debate has all the ferocity of one of Ryokan's grass fights with village children. Convention suggests that senryu deal solely with human nature, while Mother Nature is the exclusive domain of haiku. The works of Patricia Benedict and Joanne Morcom dance lively on and around this fence.

Patricia shows us that we distinguish human nature from Mother Nature at our own peril:

cloudy day –
my Harlequin pages
flutter in the wind

In their essence, there is no difference between the pages of a Harlequin romance and that of, say, an autumn leaf. Our frailties and experience as human beings, however, tell us something quite different. Patricia won't spell it out for us, though the truth of the moment makes it quite clear.

There are rather ominous implications when we combine human frailties with the notion that everything changes. These are skilfully brought out in the works of Joanne Morcom:

spring thaw
the river gives up
another body

Joanne honors the traditions of haiku while at the same time conjuring up images of our earthly end. Once again, we are only given the select facts of a particular experience or moment, but we as readers and participants are allowed to come to those rather obvious, ominous conclusions on our own.

No less true of life than its inevitable end (a truth Joanne won't let her fellow poets comfortably ignore), is its liveliness and innocence, as we find in the haiku of Lesley Dahl. Lesley draws our attention to tap-dancing socks, singing sparrows and the shared passage of time at either end of a kite string:

kite flying
slowly I unravel
the day

One could say that one place where the paths of the ascetic and of aesthetics meet is in the neighborhood of simplicity. Haiku are beautiful because they are little packets of simple truths. It's true that freedom isn't something that might happen later or elsewhere, but exists in the everyday interactions we have with our surroundings and with each other.

grey dandelions
tremble more in this fall breeze
than the yellow ones

The Magpie Haiku Poets have invested a bit of energy into a few of these interactions, and we are happy that you have decided to as well.

Tim Sampson

PATRICIA BENEDICT

Patricia Benedict (B.F.A., M.F.A.) is a retired Drama Professor who taught at the University of Calgary for sixteen years. She's been acting and writing since her teens.

She began writing haiku in the 1980's, submitting her work to journals and contests, and was delighted when her work was published.

She finds that being "in the moment" as an actor very akin to being "in the moment" when writing haiku, as both art forms demand strong focus, a dedication to truth, and a simplicity in the telling of the tale.

Patricia and her husband, Chuck, live in Calgary with their lively terrier named Keltie.

garbage dump –
spindly sunflower stands,
head bowed

autumn wake –
moon-painted shadows
fill her lifeless cheek

through the blizzard
a small boy marches
shouldering an icicle

heavy snowfall –
the sun umbrella
tips over

wind gusts –
on barbed-wire fence
a moth, fluttering

heavy snowfall –
garbage dump becomes
the local ski hill

bus delays –
angry man karate-chops
a tree

smoke-filled sky –
blackened trees surround
the empty playground

panting she lies there –
body covered with new snow,
my contented dog

watching the stars –
my dog sleeps on my foot,
my foot sleeps

stained glass sunlight –
baby's head adorned
with crown of gold

Seniors menu –
smaller portions,
bigger print

outside the church
a white feather trampled
by rushing feet

empty subway station –
footsteps on the stair
not mine…

broken eaves –
coffee cans swallowing
winter runoff

sunny washday –
Mother chatting by the fence –
we steal her shoe

after rain –
two magpies taking turns
preening in a hubcap

cloudy day –
my Harlequin pages
flutter in the wind

holiday train –
small boys wave and moon us
as we pass

movie set –
'dead' men rise
and go for lunch

DEVAR DAHL

DeVar is a school teacher in Magrath, Alberta. He was born in Edmonton, but has lived most of his life in Magrath except for a few years in Scotland, France and England. He discovered "real" haiku when he connected with haiku lists on the Internet. For several years, he has served as the Alberta, Saskatchewan and Manitoba regional coordinator with Haiku Canada. He is married to Lesley and they frequently go into the country or to the mountains to look for haiku inspiration. He has recently created an official website for Haiku Canada.

the road home
swallows fly out
both sides of the bridge

empty cabin
the beached canoe
fills with leaves

dry leaves
trapped in the spokes
grandpa's bike

small town
an old dog stops traffic
both ways

my best moo
all the cows
stop and look

it's not swearing
it's the only language
those cows understand

summer heat
the crickets wait
for me to pass

pencil shavings
the student's tongue
curls and uncurls

empty swallow nests
yellow leaves blow
into the creek

autumn sunset
the ripe rose hip
begins to pucker

a silent magpie
flies across the valley –
leafless willow

long week
a firebug walks
the rim of a glass

easter snow
a piece of egg shell
in the sandwich

midday sun
the silence of swimming
under water

sultry day
a swallow runs its beak
across the pond

homemade bread
a pound of butter
softens by the stove

loved ones return home
a harvest moon rises
over the bridge

morning dew
the horse's tail
brushes the grass

the narrow place
between my neck and my collar
November wind

prairie wind
snow fills the mouth
of the badger hole

34

LESLEY DAHL

Lesley was born in Patna, India. She lived in
England and Montreal until attending university
in the USA. Her greatest world contributions
are a joyful marriage to her husband DeVar,
and having the opportunity to raise five children
to adulthood. She is trying to shift her Western
mind to a simpler perspective, and she finds
that haiku gives her the opportunity to live
more fully in the moment.

frozen air
paired socks tap dance
on the clothesline

talking to myself
one red maple leaf
stops it all

hospice patient
above her bed a spider
suspended by a thread

 burning leaves
whispered prayers and smoke
rise on the wind

abandoned schoolhouse
a horned owl stares
through the broken window

moonless winter night
a candle in the window
melts open the ice

bareheaded scarecrow
his hat in the pumpkin patch
covers a bald spot

November wind
all around the bird feeder
only scattered seeds

kite flying
slowly I unravel
the day

summer rain
sparrows sing happily
under the birdbath

early summer
faint bell sounds
along the trail

child's lemonade stand
each plastic cup displays
a garnish of dust

south wind
blending lilacs and laundry
at my kitchen door

river bend
the setting sun catches
my imitation fly

worn past repair
grandma's feather quilt
spring sun adds a patch

sun and clouds
travel together
both sides of the fence

44

beside the grave
one set of footprints
filling with snow

corporate chatter
my office voice-mail could use
some heavy breathing

JEAN JORGENSEN

Jean, a retired nurse, comes from an Alberta farming background and got used to having nature as part of her world. After years of writing rhymed and free verse, as well as short stories, she began writing haiku and related poetry in 1987. Happily, publication has been widespread. Her work appears in several anthologies and she has published six books.

Being a wife and mother has brought Jean a lot of satisfaction, but poetry, certainly, is the something "extra" she has always been grateful for. Her fondest wish is to be remembered for these accomplishments, through her three adult children and her haiku poems.

hundreds of waxwings
descend on the mountain ash
berries seem to go... like that!

a woodpecker clings
to an ice-covered branch
sundog "round" the sun

beside
the outdoor crèche
plastic Santa

her chronic illness
the fanciest Christmas card
from the pharmacist

hoarfrost shimmers down
as sparrows change perches
sparkle of her ring

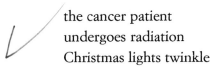
the cancer patient
undergoes radiation
Christmas lights twinkle

small coastal town
price of an ice cream cone
big city

small town mall
the retired folk drift past
tables of antiques

new calendar
absently... she flips ahead
to spring

in the snow
cat tracks
circle around the old car
... disappear

cucumber slices
on her puffy eyelids
her perfectly manicured hands

with a smile
waitress hands us our coffee
'leaded' and 'unleaded'

she sucks in
the tingle of cool air
... menthol cough-drop

evening walk
north wind swirls the snow
... his greying hair

lost… twice
all that lovely scenery
we would have missed

our empty yard
the croak of a magpie
as it circles away

they seem to drift
out of waning moonlight
snow clouds

sister's house
newly renovated
crumbling marriage

oleander in bloom
along the Texas freeway
smell of exhaust

friend wipes her face
on the veranda
bread dough rising

JOANNE MORCOM

Joanne writes and publishes haiku, tanka, haibun, visual poems (eyeku), flash fiction, essays and articles. She's attracted to haiku's deceptive simplicity, sharp imagery and subtle insights. Besides her affiliation with the Magpie Haiku Poets, she's a member of Haiku Canada and the Society of Poets, Bards and Storytellers, which organizes the annual Calgary Poets' Stroll.

A social worker by profession, she and her husband Wayne live in Calgary with their cat Roxy. Joanne collects quotations, including this one by Thomas Mann: "A writer is somebody for whom writing is more difficult than it is for other people." And she agrees with William S. Burroughs who said that paranoia is having all the facts.

spring thaw
the river gives up
another body

passion play
I watch the crucifixion
through binoculars

AA meeting
eyes watering
from cigarette smoke

ladybug
on a blade of grass
up, down, around

surrounding
the quiet bungalow
yellow crime scene tape

buffalo jump
the sound of crickets
and a hot wind

July dawn
magpies in the school yard
play a game

midway lights
the carnival worker's
glass eye

autumn dusk
a leaf pile stirs
resettles

misty moon
the cemetery gate
opens

the old corral
corrals
a snow drift

winter night
I keep the telemarketer
talking

throughout
the blizzard… soft click
of knitting needles

Christmas Eve
the wino mumbles
a carol

feeling cranky
the palm reader tells him
she's never seen
a life line
as short as his

crash, bang, boom
goes the midnight thunder
I snuggle closer to you
and then remember
you don't live here anymore

BERRYMAN
  I
  V
  E
  R

O
CRANE
E
A
N

  L
  A
  K
SHELLEY

TIM SAMPSON

After getting his B.Sc. and B.Ed., Tim started
to pursue some rather clichéd archetypes.
A few years were spent as an obsessive long-
distance runner, a few as an anti-car/pro-bike
activist, and a few in a Zen temple trying to
break through the trap of clichéd archetypes.
While stuck in the Zen archetype in a
monastery in Northern England, Tim met Bill
Wyatt, an accomplished haiku poet, who
started him on this latest... well... pursuit. Tim
lives in Calgary and currently works in the
world of second-hand books.

finished
with a January dumpster –
the tinselled cat

through the poplars
a spruce tree
full of snow

grey dandelions
tremble more in this fall breeze
than the yellow ones

enough room
between the gravestones
barrow full of leaves

stopping
to hear a starling
finish

bad-mouthing a wasp –
nearly swallow
an aphid

clothes peg
clothes peg chickadee
clothes peg clothes peg

between stops –
the bus doors open
for a bee

yard sale –
the neighbor's dog
exhausted

sparrows have flown
to some further poplars –
so I sing louder

into the path
of a pick-up truck –
two green moths

squinting through the snow
to see if ducks
squint

robins interrupt
robins interrupting –
spring hedgerow

behind the thrift store –
a California Raisin's
armless head

the kind of snow
that sticks for a bit
to a magpie's foot

St. Francis
wants a word with you
Brother Magpie

open convertible –
the brims of their straw hats
overlap

a pigeon pecks
at a cigarette butt –
then another

floating somewhere
in this autumn snow –
downy aspen seeds

let's walk this way –
it'll take a bit longer
but we'll see some ducks

NOTES

Some of the haiku in this anthology have appeared in the following print and electronic publications. Permission to reprint in this collection is given by the authors.

Patricia Benedict

"garbage dump" in *Haiku Canada Newsletter,* Vol. XVI, February 2003, ed. LeRoy Gorman

"autumn walk" in *Ontario Poetry Society,* Vol. 2, No. 2, December 2001, ed. I.B. Iskov

"moon-painted shadows" in *Sandburg-Livesay Anthology,* 1999; and in *Electronic Poetry Network,* November 24, 2003, ed. Carlos Colon

"sunny washday" in *RAW NerVZ,* VIII:2, summer, 2003, ed. Dorothy Howard; and in *we steal her shoe,* 2002, ed. Bruce Ross

"cloudy day" in *Ashai Haikuist Network*, August 2003, ed. David McMurray

"movie set" in *Haiku Canada Newsletter*, May 2003, ed. LeRoy Gorman

DeVar Dahl

"the road home" in *pawEpress 58*, ed. LeRoy Gorman

"empty cabin" in *Snapshot Press Haiku Calendar,* 2002

"dry leaves", "small town", "my best moo" and "it's not swearing" in *Between the Clouds*, Red Iron Press, 2003

"summer heat" in *Haiku Canada Newsletter,* Vol. 14, No. 3, ed. LeRoy Gorman "empty swallow nests" in *Presence No. 14,* May 2001

"easter snow" in *Presence No. 17,* May 2002

"midday sun" in *WHC World Haiku Review,* Vol. 1, No. 3

"sultry day" and "homemade bread" in *WHC World Haiku Review* Vol. 1, No. 3

"homemade bread" in WHC *World Haiku Review* Vol. 3, No. 2

"loved ones return home" in *Shimanami Kaido/99 Contest* (third place)

"morning dew" and "the narrow place" in *Snapshot Press Haiku Calendar 2003*

"the farmer's spit" in *The Heron's Nest,* Vol. 4, No.11

Lesley Dahl

"kite flying" in *International Kusamakura Haiku Contest* (second place), 2002

Joanne Morcom

"passion play" in *Haiku Canada Newsletter,* Vol. XVI, No. 2, February 2003, ed. LeRoy Gorman

"AA meeting" in *Beyond Spring Rain: Haiku Canada's 25th Members' Anthology, 2001-2002,* ed. LeRoy Gorman

"surrounding" in *RAW NerVZ III:1,* Spring 1996, ed. Dorothy Howard; and in *The Haiku Anthology,* W.W. Norton & Company, 1999, ed. Cor van den Heuvel; and in *pawEpress,* October 1999, ed. LeRoy Gorman

"midway lights" in *Asahi Haikuist Network,* August 11, 2003, ed. David McMurray "autumn dusk" in *The Electronic Poetry Network*, October 9, 2003, ed. Carlos Colon

"the old corral" in *The Haiku Hundred*, Iron Press, 1992, ed. James Kirkup, David Cobb, Peter Mortimer

"winter night" in *tinywords haiku contest* (fourth place), April 2003

"throughout the blizzard" in *pale moon Haiku Canada Sheet*, 2000, ed. LeRoy Gorman

"Christmas Eve" in *Frogpond*, vol. X, No. 4, November 1987, ed. Elizabeth Searle Lamb; and in *pawEpress*, October 1999, ed. Leroy Gorman

"feeling cranky" and "crash, bang, boom" in *Tanka Splendor 1994: Mirrors 5th International Tanka Awards*, AHA Books, ed. Jane Reichhold; and in *Full Moon Tide*, 2001, ed. Linda Jeannette Ward, and in *Countless Leaves: North American Tanka Contest 2001*, Inkling Press, ed. Gerald St. Maur

Tim Sampson

"robins interrupt", "the kind of snow", and "let's walk this way" in *chirp*, 2001, ed. Bruce Ross

"squinting through the snow" in *we steal her shoe*, 2002, ed. Bruce Ross

ACKNOWLEDGEMENTS

We would like to thank the following people for helping to make this anthology possible: Bruce Ross for starting us on our way and providing the Foreword, John Vickers for his design and layout work, Jim Harding and Author! Author! Books for technical support, Romana Prokopiw for her editing skills and Ken Richardson for his artwork.

For more information about the group contact magpiehaiku@hotmail